The Lotus

By

Catherine Campbell

Dedicated to:

My beautiful friend, Tanya

- your unwavering belief in me is why I'm here.

"No mud, no lotus."

[Thich Nhat Hanh]

Introduction

Buddhists live by the philosophy, "No mud, no lotus." Those four simple words effortlessly convey the human experience. I've long been in love with the symbolism attached to the lotus flower, so to be privileged in using its image to accompany my poetry feels like bringing an old friend with me on the journey.

Just as the lotus seed comes to life in murky swamp water, snarled with roots, I believe human beings are born into a world that isn't entirely fit-for-purpose or supportive of their personal growth. Over time, though we've made transformative advances in industry and technology, in parallel the world seems to have become increasingly chaotic, leaving many of us dazed by distraction. Our attention is drawn every which way, as though we're puppets on a string, while the profit masters compete relentlessly for a slice of it.

Human beings are millennia away from having evolved to adapt to the world we've created, but this is the world they're now born into. I'm less inclined to applaud giant leaps of humankind as I've become more acutely aware of the collateral damage left in its wake, such as our loss of connectivity as humans, and the reason we're alive at all.

Each one of us is a complex and beautiful being, with real feelings. At the end of the day, we're all in this together, doing the best we can to muddle through the murky waters of life.

A lotus's journey into the light is not for the feint hearted. It draws strength while in the darkness, from an unshakeable belief there *is* light, and no challenge is too great to dampen its desire to reach it. This is the journey a human must also take if they desire transcendence from society's tangled roots and expectations.

While we speak different languages and are born into different cultures and circumstances, some experiences are universal to us all. At some point in our lives, we will all experience love, joy, sadness, loss, and death. Emotions speak a universal language every human can understand. Emotions unite us and offer an opportunity for us to feel compassion and empathy towards each other. Our growth as humans doesn't come from giant leaps in technology. It comes from being exposed to these experiences at a personal level, permitting ourselves to be vulnerable as they consume us, and having the courage to share our feelings with others in order to deepen connection. Every time we do that, we become a little more resilient than before, a little closer to the light.

All my life, poetry has been my companion. It has never failed to comfort me though love and loss. It was, and continues to be, my trusted counsel through both the joys and challenges of motherhood, where it has never offered judgement.

Now, as I'm consciously navigating towards a simpler, less chaotic life, it continues to be my source of calm. The poems in this book all stem from my own experiences. In sharing, I hope some of the words will resonate and serve as a reminder we're all human, and in this life together.

I'm very grateful you are here. Thank you.

Catherine Campbell

Table of Contents

Life

The Swan

Above the surface, I am a swan.
Almost mystical,
projecting elegance and tranquillity,
regally floating through the tides of my life
such that I appear untouchable.

Above the surface, I am a swan.
Almost mythical,
projecting poise and grace,
effortlessly adapting to my surroundings
such that I appear unflappable.

Above the surface, I am a swan.
Almost magical,
projecting strength and speed,
fiercely protective of my mate & cygnets
such that I appear unconditional.

Beneath the surface, I am also a swan.
Almost agitated,
exhibiting inelegance and chaos,
fervently flapping through the tides of my life
such that I appear incapable.

Beneath the surface, I am also a swan.
Almost aggressive,
exhibiting frustration and imbalance,
tenaciously treading through circumstance
such that I appear impassive.

Beneath the surface, I am also a swan.
Almost arrogant,
exhibiting pride and determination,
painstakingly paddling to keep up appearances,
such that I appear impenetrable.

Beneath the surface, a monumental effort goes into the
projection of effortlessness above the surface.

Some have only ever loved the top half of me.
Very few have braved the deep dive,
or been prepared to hold their breath long enough,
to reach the depth of me.

To those who have, thank you.
You are my calm.

Unspoken Words

Where do words go if we don't speak them –

if they never fall from the lips of those who ache to say them?
or upon the ears of those who long to hear them?

They are swept under a rug,
only to be found lying there, still,
when the rug is pulled from under you.

They are drowned at sea,
only to float upon the shore once more,
when the synergy of moon and tides is just so.

They are thrown to the wind,
only to come full circle and land at your feet,
though you'd walked a million miles beyond them.

They are chewed and swallowed,
only to choke you when you least expect it.

Why do we abandon words, even as they risk the journey
from our hearts to our mouths?

What are we afraid of?
What if they are the most important words of all?

"Between what is said and not meant,

and what is meant and not said,

most of love is lost."

[Khalil Gibran]

Brief Encounter

Today I held the elevator door open for an elderly man.

He approached in slow motion, as quick as his fragile body would allow, though a sense of urgency flickered in his eyes when he looked up and saw the opening suspended for his arrival.

With a flash of determination, his pace quickened.

He shuffled in, with a muffled, "Thank you."

"My pleasure," I replied.

We didn't meet each other's eyes.

In the time it took to elevate to the 9th floor, I resisted an urge to reach towards him and hug him.

I wanted to hold his eyes and say,

"I know you.

"You're a human being, just like me, only we're wearing different bodies."

I wanted to say,

"I can see you've lived far longer on our earth than me. How has your life been?

"I hope it's been happy.

"I hope people have been kind to you."

I wanted to say,

"I love you."

But I didn't.

I didn't say any of that.

Instead, we arrived at the 9th floor, and I held the door open
for him to leave.

And he shuffled out, with a muffled, "Thank you."

Space

In space, I feel.

Music is meaningless without the silence between notes.
Anticipation dwells there...
how my pulse quickens in that space -
how my soul aches to embrace what comes next.

Art is shallow in the absence of space.
Perspective dwells there...
how my eyes are soothed by what is uncluttered -
how my mind is seduced into appreciating it's depth.

A novel is unstructured without breakpoints.
Contemplation dwells there...
how my breath catches with a chapter's climax -
how my heart rests in swollen silence at its end.

Communication is thoughtless without pause.
Responsiveness dwells there...
how my ears devour what is left unspoken -
how my voice rises to conquer vulnerability when invited.

Life itself exists in our pause between breaths.
For in that space,
if our body is willing...
we are gifted to draw another.

"A seed grows with no sound,
but a tree falls with huge noise.
Destruction has noise, but creation is quiet.
This is the power of silence.
Grow silently."

[Confutus]

Out of Body Experience

Do you ever feel, sometimes...
like you want to peel off your body
and gently step out of it,
as though it were a onesie...

Then lower it carefully to the floor,
in the corner of your room,
and walk around naked for a while?

I do, sometimes.

I don't know what naked feels like without a body,
but I imagine it must be very liberating.

Leaving Home

She packed her things and took her leave,
with wings on feet and heart on sleeve -
then cast a final glance of home.
renouncing warmly, all she'd known.

She left what she could live without -
the heaviness of fear and doubt.
As optimism held her hand,
she ventured to the promised land.

She travelled wide, and journeyed far,
fixated on her Northern Star.
Tomorrows turned to yesterday,
as perseverance paved her way.

Eventually, each end in sight,
transpired to be a trick of light.
Despite the distance gone before,
the path extended, ever more.

The wings had fallen from her feet,
her heart dis-heartened with defeat.
Her compass flailed from east to west...
exhausted, she took pause to rest.

And there in stillness, peace was born,
awakening her soul to dawn.
A self-awareness settled in...
she'd find her promised land within.

Without regret for all she'd learned,
while navigating twists and turns,
she moved illusive goals aside,
and set her course to source, inside.

Who Cares

There's a woman in the doorway,
her hair a mottled grey,
positioned for a penny in the startling light of day.

Her cardboard reads, "Please help me.
"I don't have much to eat."
An empty bottle lying at her naked, blackened feet.

Her pillow is a cotton bag,
which bulges at its seams,
possessions she has clung to in the wake of broken dreams.

Her sleeping bag hangs threadbare,
and cloaks her bony frame,
her eyes avoid all contact; her head is hung in shame.

Of 1000's of commuters,
who daily pass her by,
no-one dares to lift her face or look her in the eye.

No-one thinks to help her,
despite her cardboard plea -
they swiftly fix their gaze ahead, disturbed by what they see.

Maybe all she really needs,
is just for one to care –
just one, to meet her pleading eyes,
and ask who left her there.

Unplugged

Some days,
I wish I didn't have to be here.
Not in a life and death way…
in an unplugged, disconnected way.

In a way where no energy can be drawn from me -
where there's no expectation for me to be a source of light,
or to shine.

I could just be a candle,
free to flicker in my own atmosphere,
- or not.

My burning out wouldn't impact anyone else.
I could simply be still, and quiet in the darkness -
and that would be perfectly OK.
I would be perfectly comfortable being that.

When I felt ready,
I could catch the next spark,
and ignite again.

My flame would glow a little brighter,
reach a little higher,
and flicker a little steadier than before.

I would feel more alive,
more energised, ironically,
having been unplugged.

"Solitude is a silent storm that breaks down all
our dead branches; yet sends our living roots
deeper into the living heart of the living earth."

[Kahlil Gibran]

Equal Measure

I have allowed grief and sorrow to grip my heart.
Unapologetically,
with such reckless abandon and ferocity,
I believed I might die.

In *equal measure* -

I have allowed beauty and joy to grip my heart.
Unapologetically,
with such reckless abandon, and ferocity,
I believed I might die.

Is it a curse,
or a blessing -
to feel so recklessly and ferociously,
at times one feels one's own call to death?

Superwoman

I'm a very busy woman,
we can't do that today -
there's more to life than fun & games,
I don't have time to play.

I'm a very conscious eater,
you won't find any sweets -
my meals are full of nutrients,
I don't indulge in treats.

I'm a very classy dresser,
so don't suggest the hat -
I'm mindful how my style projects,
I can't be seen in that.

I'm a very honest worker,
sit still, and let me rule -
my reputation's paramount,
I'll not be made a fool.

I'm a very active woman,
we can't just lay about -
my mother always told me,
"If it's nice outside, GET OUT!"

I'm a super proper person,
so please... just don't react -
I pride myself on etiquette,
and must remain intact.

I'm a Very Boring Woman.

Wait. What?

I'm. A. Very. Boring. Woman.

I didn't mean to be like this,
it doesn't feel like me -
it's not the way I was before,
or how I want to be.

So, who have I been talking to,
this child, who interferes?

It's ME -
she's come to rescue me,
she's been there, all these years.

Ethereal Balance

It's fundamental.

When there is light on one side of the planet,
there is darkness on the other.

A seed must lie beneath the earth in darkness,
before it can emerge, miraculously, into the light.

There is no trying required, in this process of emergence.

There is no room for wishing it would happen any sooner
that it does.

It just happens. So too it is in life -

Where there is darkness, there will be light.

Only in embracing our darkness,
can we ever truly appreciate our light.

Where there is sorrow, there will be joy.

Only in having felt crushed by sorrow,
can we truly measure the weightlessness of our joy.

Where there is grief, there will be love.

Only in having been paralysed by grief,
can we truly appreciate the value of our love.

Where there is depression, there will be life.

Only having known the apathy,
the desolateness,
the choke of whispering smoke
rising from the embers of a tortured soul...

Only then,
can we truly recognise
the spark,
the glow of hope,
the trembling courage it takes to believe
a fire might blaze again,
the euphoria of feeling oneself draw breath again.

It's fundamental.

Love

Mother's Love

I Get It

The day my son came inside out,
it altered me, without a doubt -
and rather unexpectedly,
my heart crashed through the wall of me.

His day of birth, I changed somehow.
I get it, Mum.
I get it now.

The day he broke his fragile bone,
I felt it crack, as if my own -
and rather understandably,
I wished his pain belonged to me.

It wasn't fair on him, somehow.
I get it, Mum.
I get it now.

The day he walked to school alone,
like MI5, I tracked him home -
I acted calm, but secretly,
relief swept through the veins of me.

I took that leap of faith, somehow.
I get it, Mum.
I get it now.

The day he learned to drive a car,
I hoped he wouldn't venture far -
and rather uncontrollably,
a cloak of fear fell over me.

He felt too young to drive, somehow.
I get it, Mum.
I get it now.

The day his lover broke his heart,
I felt my own had ripped apart.
Instinctively, protectively,
I longed to wrap him up in me.

I had to ease his pain, somehow.
I get it, Mum.
I get it now.

The day he flew from feathered nest,
my heart launched with him, from my chest.
I felt alone, but equally,
a swell of pride washed over me.

I'd helped him learn to fly, somehow.
I get it, Mum.
I get it now.

Mum, you told me, as I grew,
I'd need my own, before I knew…
you'd squeeze me gently by the hand,
and say, "One day, you'll understand."

I get it, Mum,
I really do.

And Mum, at last,
I get you too.

Through the Years

At one
I carried you.
I took you everywhere I went.
You were my unconditional little cuddle buddy -
the absolute centre of my world.
I loved you fiercely.

At five
I held your hand.
I let you go in good faith, enabling you to wander cautiously,
yet freely into your first magnificent solo adventures.
I loved you fiercely.

At ten
I encouraged you.
I helped you find your own little light,
and showed you how to keep it shining.
even when others tried to blow it out.
I loved you fiercely.

At fifteen
I watched you.
I became a shadow, observing you from a distance,
like a hawk ready to swoop the second I thought
you were in trouble -

trying so very hard to glide about nonchalantly,
and not swoop in by accident.
I loved you fiercely.

At eighteen
I empowered you.
I assisted you on your way,
then watched with tremendous pride,
as you left confidently to begin the rest of your life.
I loved you fiercely.

At twenty
You don't need me to carry you anymore -
you carry yourself just beautifully.

You don't need me to hold your hand anymore -
though I hope you'll always have someone in your life
who will.

You don't need me to encourage you anymore -
your light is blazing, and everyone can see it.

You don't need me to watch over you anymore -
I trust you'll find me if you're ever in trouble.

You don't need me to empower you anymore -
because you know in your heart how capable you are.

You don't *need* me to do any of these things for you now -
but know this... I would.

In a heartbeat.

Because I love you fiercely.

Days of Motherhood

I didn't hold your hand that day.
Because,
while I was on a mission, you were dawdling...
paying extraordinary attention to the ants
crawling into pavement cracks,
without consideration for my schedule.

So frustrating.

I'm sorry darling.
I dawdle sometimes too now, and it would be nice for
someone to hold my hand, without trying to rush me.

I asked you to stop talking that day.
Because,
while I was craving silence, you were babbling...
incessantly speaking loudly your every thought
to anyone who would listen,
without consideration for my sanity.

So aggravating.

I'm sorry darling.
I speak my thoughts out loud sometimes too now,
and love it when people listen, without interruption.

I told you I wouldn't play a game with you that day.
Because,
while I was busy, you were bored...
interrupting me constantly, only interested
in entertaining yourself,
without consideration for my agenda.

So irritating.

I'm sorry darling.
I get bored sometimes too now and would love nothing
more than to play a game with you, without time restriction.

I asked you to go away and leave me alone that day.
Because,
while I needed space, you needed company...
following me around, jumping all over me, smothering me,
without consideration for my personal space.

So agitating.

I'm sorry darling.
I have all the space I need now, and would love nothing
more than your company, without conditions.

When you're a mother,
some days *are* -
frustrating, aggravating, and irritating.

Those days were difficult.

However,
there were vastly more days,
my love,
when we *did* hold hands,
and share thoughts,
and play games,
and cuddle.

Those days were the best days of my life.

To Whom It May Concern

A father gives away the bride; his daughter - duty done.
I wonder when a mother, then,
should give away her son?

I'd like to give my son away with more than just a kiss.
And so, *To Whom He Gives Himself*,
to You, I give you this -

I give to you his ocean eyes,
which first gazed into mine.
I give to you his mark of birth,
uniquely our design.

I give to you his graceful hands,
which tucked in mine for years.
I give to you his battle scars,
each carved from childhood tears.

I give to you his gifted mind,
which learned to read with ease.
I give to you his outstretched arms,
which brought me to my knees.

I give to you his open wings,
which launched him from my nest.
I give to you his tender heart,
which beats outside his chest.

I give to you his little light,
now blazing from his soul.
I give in faith, his mother's heart -
the first he ever stole.

He'll always be my little boy,
for all the days l live.
So, this I ask with all I have,
please cherish all I give.

Lover's Love

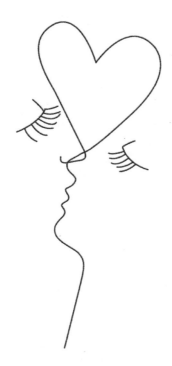

I Need Nothing But

I don't need you to take me to an exclusive restaurant...
but bring me tea in bed,
steaming from my beautiful floral cup,
and I'm *Yours*.

I don't need you to buy me expensive flowers...
but pick me a wildflower as we meander
down the road less travelled,
and I'm *Yours*.

I don't need you to adorn me with a gold ring...
but find a beautiful shell on the beach,
carved by the tides, and slip it on my finger,
and I'm *Yours*.

I don't need you to whisk me away to a luxury retreat...
but pack us a lazy rug and picnic,
and lay it down where the birds sing,
and I'm *Yours*.

I don't need you to move mountains for me...
but take me to a place where we can spend all day mooning
at them in their magnificent glory,
and I'm *Yours*.

I don't need you to chase the end of a rainbow for me...
but recognise the gold is already where we stand,
and I'm *Yours*.

Rising in Love

What an odd expression it is,
to say one *falls* in love -
to imply one is lowered; less, somehow.

Is it not more fitting.
more hopeful,
to say one *rises* in love...
to imply one may become greater -
that one might ascend to heights unknown?

Coming Together

I've carried you in my heart,
since the notion of love first dawned upon me.

In quiet times, when I longed for comfort in a world I didn't
fit into, I'd close my eyes and find you.

The warmth of your presence softened my edges.

The strength of our connection felt more real than anything
I'd ever felt, eyes wide open.

Our love was a rare and beautiful escape.

While I was adrift from the shore of a shallow reality,
I was anchored and safe with you in the deep.

Most dismissed me as a dreamer.

But always, I carried you in my heart.
I'd never met you,
but I knew you'd find me too, one day.
I trusted us.

Before we met, I offered my heart to others,
but never completely.
I was unable to allow access to the space reserved for you -
the room in wait, not yet furnished with our love.

It took 40 years to find you darling, and our love is
everything I knew it would be.

The warmth of your presence softens my edges.

The strength of our connection *is* real,

We are anchored, and safe together in the deep.

Our eyes are wide open,
and this is not a dream.

Self-Love

When life lays down its sword,
Leaving you defeated,
only you, can fill the void; restore what's been depleted.

Smell the nearest roses,
dress in something bright,
love yourself so crushingly, you're dazzled by its might.

Put away your cell phone,
catch yourself some breeze,
love yourself so tenderly, you're weakened at the knees.

Eat forbidden baking,
play your favourite songs,
love yourself so graciously, you're sifted from your wrongs.

Lift your face to sunlight,
fill your lungs with air,
love yourself so fearlessly, your spirit rises bare.

Find a place of stillness,
gift your thoughts release,
love yourself so patiently, you're wrapped with inner peace.

Do what pulls your heart strings,
do what stirs your soul,
fill yourself with all this love, until you come back whole.

"Let there be spaces in your togetherness and let the winds
of the heavens dance between you.
Love one another but make not a bond of love:
Let it rather be a moving sea,
between the shores of your souls.

Fill each other's cup but drink not from one cup.
Give one another of your bread,
but eat not from the same loaf.

Sing and dance together and be joyous, but let each one of
you be alone, even as the strings of a lute are alone though
they quiver with the same music.

Give your hearts, but not into each other's keeping, for only
the hand of Life can contain your hearts.

And stand together, yet not too near together:
For the pillars of the temple stand apart, and the oak tree
and the cypress grow not in each other's shadow."

[Kahlil Gibran]

I Can't Say I Love You

I can't tell you how much I love you,
or how grateful I am for you.
I can't find the words,
literally.

Nothing in our language seems adequate -
no matter how magnificently
I attempt to string words together.

I feel I'd have to invent some new ones -
like perhaps *ultramorious*,
or *euphanoria*.

Then I could say something like,
I am *ultramoriously euphanoristic* about you.

But even that seems inadequate.

The thing about love -
it's a *feeling*.

It's how you make me feel.

I think one could speak until the clocks fall off the wall,
in a valiant effort to express love –

but words are merely water striders.

Feelings brave the deep.

You'll just have to trust me when I say,
I can't tell you how much I love you.

Little Things

Silky sheets and satin slips,
gifts with Midas touch -
lavish weekend whisk-always,
it's all a bit too much.

It's not that I'm ungrateful,
but this will never do...
little things are all I need to fall in love with you.

Serenades and sunset shores,
robes of silken touch -
lilies wrapped in golden bows,
it's all a bit too much.

It's not that I'm ungrateful,
but this will never do...
little things are all I need to fall in love with you.

Little things -
like hold my hand,
and walk with me a while.

Little things –
like catch my eye,
and share a knowing smile.

Little things –
like sit me down,
and make my favourite tea.

Little things –
like wish me luck,
and say you'll think of me.

Little things –
like kiss my brow,
and soothe me when I'm ill.

Little things –
like when I'm old,
I'll feel you love me still.

It's little things that matter,
for love is not to strive…
little things are seeds of love -
from little things, we'll thrive.

What I Really Mean

You know you're the love of my life, right?
When you're not with me and in the morning, I say,
"I hope you have a good day love,"
what I really mean is –

I hope you take some time for yourself to replenish.
Because you and I are sunflowers,
who turn to each other to recharge.
And sunflowers on their own can wither without warning.

I hope you keep appreciating the little things.
Because you and I find joy in flowers, and shells,
and drinking tea from beautiful cups.
These are magical little things.

I hope you keep the twinkle in your eyes,
and the playfulness in your soul.

I hope your heart swells and your body moves,
when you hear your favourite songs.

I hope the people around you are making you feel happy,
and you're smiling a lot.

I hope you are well,
and safe,
because I need you to come home to me, as you were.

That's what I really mean.

When you're not with me and in the evening, I say,
"Sleep well, darling,"
what I really mean is –

I hope your day was all the things I'd hoped it would be,
and you go to bed happy.

I hope nothing is worrying you, that might keep you awake.

I hope you can feel my spirit embracing you,
and imagine my touch as you drift to sleep.

I hope if you remember your dreams, they are beautiful,
and you wake wrapped in the comfort of knowing
how much you are loved.

I hope you'll be able to wake on your own agenda and have
time to drink tea from a beautiful cup,
before your day begins.

I hope you are well,
and safe,
because I need you to come home to me, as you were.

That's what I really mean.

Loss

Seasons

Darling, I'm not leaving,
the seasons never grieve.
Look to nature; trust me love, I need you to believe -

In summer,
I'm the flowers in pohutakawa trees.

In autumn,
I'll be drifting in kaleidoscopic leaves.

In winter,
I'm the little spark that keeps your fire aglow.

In springtime,
you will find me where the gladioli grow.

Darling, I'm not leaving,
I'll always be in view.
Look to nature; trust me love, I'm everywhere, with you.

My Friend

It's your laugh I miss most,
the way you tossed your head back.
All in.
That I won't hear you laugh again is inconceivable.

The way you played the piano made me feel I was melting.
All in.
That I won't hear you play again is unimaginable.

The way your tortured yourself over which clothes to wear
drove me insane... always impeccable, yet so indecisive.
All in.
That you'll never ask my opinion again is incomprehensible.

The way we found humour in everyday things –
so often we were the only two giggling.
All in.
That I won't find myself lost in goofy giddiness again with
you, is unbelievable.

The compassion you always showed towards other people,
the way you blessed and brightened their lives,
All in.
That you didn't live long enough to receive it all back is
unforgiveable.

That you are gone is:

Inconceivable

Unimaginable

Incomprehensible

Unbelievable

Unforgiveable

As you found me in friendship,
so too shall you find me in grief...
All in.

"When you are sorrowful, look again in your heart,
and you shall see that in truth,
you are weeping for that which has been your delight."

[Khalil Gibran]

Hope Sparks

There's a place beyond letting go and acceptance,
where embers of hope still glow for what might have been.

And sometimes,
though one has mastered fixing their gaze forward,
one's peripheral vision is caught –
by a flicker,
a look,
a smile.

In that moment,
everything changes.

The choking emotion
and ferocity of the fire
is forgotten…
it's memory a mere whisp of smoke.

When one's attention is drawn
by a flicker,
a look,
a smile…

hope sparks.

Make It Stop

My clock fell off the wall when you left –
what use have I for time now?

The world continues to spin around its axis with disregard,
as if nothing has changed,
when everything has.

Now I feel sick with the dizziness of it all.

If love makes the world go around,
there's little wonder death leaves us paralysed.

When I'm Gone

One day, when I am gone, while you live on -
your night will be sprinkled with the same stars
I now gaze upon.

Your body will be warmed by the same sun.

Flowers will grow as gloriously as they ever have.

Birds will still chirp delightfully on spring mornings,
as if only for you,
as they did for me.

One day, when I am gone, while you live on -
you will look out to the same sea,
existing as it always has, in its expansive, glistening glory.

You will make the same journeys and drive the same roads.

You will lay your eyes upon the very same mountains
I once did.
The very same trees will filter the light and shade your
journey, each now little fuller, a little closer to the sky.

One day, when I am gone, while you live on –
our paths will cross in countless ways,
and I will be - *always* - where you are.

Leave a Light On

Darling, leave a light on,
but don't wait up for me.
I've no way of knowing (or how far I'm going)
but for all we know…

I'll have wings on the other side,
and as a moth is drawn from darkness
towards the glow of a solitary lantern,
so too shall I be drawn to you,
my love.

Light

Don't Turn Around

I've always been a hurried walker,
stubbornly determined to outrun my own shadow.
I just needed to leap that bit further to get past it -
darkness would be no companion of mine.

Eyes ahead,
forward bound,
never trip or turn around.

I've always been a fastidious planner,
intensely driven to meet perfection at the horizon.
I just needed to get close enough to look her in the eye,
ask her how it feels to be so desired.

Eyes ahead,
forward bound,
never trip or turn around.

I've always been an idealistic dreamer,
steadfastly focused on reaching the oasis
I anticipated would replenish me.
I just needed to stop ingesting society's hallucinogens,
so I could walk an unwavering path,
rather than stagger under their influence.

Eyes ahead,
forward bound,
never trip or turn around.

I've always been:

Hurried, and stubbornly determined.

Fastidious, and intensely driven.

Idealistic, and steadfastly focused.

Eyes ahead,
forward bound.
Afraid to trip or turn around.

Only recently,
I noticed how exhausted I'd become,
being all these things.

So, I stopped.

When I stopped, curiosity got the better of me.
I found the courage to stare down my fear.
I turned around,
and instantly saw how far I'd come.

I saw it was *never* possible to outrun my shadow -
she will walk beside me for as long as the sun emits light.

I saw it was *never* possible to meet perfection -
the horizon is an illusion, that had me hypnotised
into searching for the end of a circle.

I saw it was *never* possible to walk a straight line
towards my oasis.
I was breastfed on social norms -
now I get to choose whether I shallow that pill.

How happy I am,
to have noticed my exhaustion.

How happy I am,
to have stopped,
turned around,
and changed my view.

Kaleidoscope Dreamer

She dreams when she is restless,
her earthly mind asleep -
her hidden mind emerging as she ventures to the deep.

The images seduce her,
as swirling hues unfold -
she slips into her other world, subconsciously betrothed.

She cloaks herself with courage,
and holds herself with grace -
her day-time mask abandoned now, so all can see her face.

While gliding through the ether,
immune to fear or flight -
she's vulnerable, yet hopeful she will meet the truth tonight.

As crystals morph to focus,
incited by her trust -
her eyes are drawn to look upon the images she must.

Revealed in what beholds her,
at last, she sees the truth -
which validates the feelings overwhelming her since youth.

She views it with compassion,
permits herself release -
and wakes to find her restless heart is finally, at peace.

Becoming

When I'm in my garden, I feel deeply connected to my
plants, as though they are an extension of me.
I can spend hours quietly loving each one and come away
knowing every inch of them.

I can sense what each one needs,
be it water, or light, or shade.

Each one is different.

Today, in my garden, I realised I am exactly like them -
that all humans are.

I immediately thought of the labels attached to plants when
you buy them, indicating how to care for them:

Prefers full sun. Slow growing to maximum height.

*Position in partial sun. Ideally, full sun in the morning,
followed by afternoon shade.*

*Grows best in shade or filtered sunlight.
Avoid direct sunlight.*

If I'd come with my own label at birth, it would have said:

Exists happily in full sun, but needs periodic shade to grow to full potential.

Throughout my life, sunlight has never extended me. On the contrary, it's my periods in the shade that have encouraged me to flourish; requiring me to use what little energy I have left to burst through to the next level.

It's the *absence* of light that has extended my growth, towards the metaphorical heights of self-awareness.

It can be very isolating in the absence of light. At times I've felt afraid, as though I've been left in a dark corner where I may never enjoy direct sunlight again.

But it's also very *quiet* there, without distraction.

That's when it happens. I stop looking to my environment for nourishment, and get back to my roots.

I remember where I came from. I have conversations with my soul. My fronds unfurl. And I become again.

Here I Stand

I'm standing at the precipice,
undaunted by its edge –
precisely where I need to be, to carry out my pledge.

I'm standing at the precipice,
my heart outside my chest –
pulsing strong, triumphantly, in honour of my quest.

I'm standing at the precipice,
with courage heaven sent -
fears abandoned by the way, to honour my intent.

I'm standing at the precipice,
my spirit set to soar –
life has brought me here today, in search of something
more.

I'm standing at the precipice,
alive in every sense -
this is where resistance ends, and freedom slays defence.

I'm standing at the precipice,
at one with earth and sky -
committed now to one more step, in faith that I will fly…

Emotional Revolution

Today, I cradled Sadness,
I met her in the eye.
"I'm leaving you," I whispered,
and urged her not to cry.

She fought with her displacement,
afraid of letting go.
"I need the space," I told her,
"So happiness to grow."

Today I held my Anger,
I gazed upon her face.
"You're fear disguised," I whispered,
"Deserving of more grace."

She felt resistance melting,
her circuitry rewired,
"Please find some space," I asked her,
"So love can come inside."

Today I hugged Forgiveness,
I took her hand in mine.
"I've searched for you," I whispered,
"You found me just in time."

She coursed throughout my blood stream,
dissolving all my pain,
"You've rescued me," I told her,
"Now peace can take her reign."

Today I kissed Elation,
alluded I was free...
asked if she might contemplate
a walk through life, with me.

She answered in an instant,
with rapture in her face...
"Yes, of course" she whispered,
"I've longed for your embrace."

Bucket List

Head, without chatter,
love, without strings -
home, without silly, superfluous things.

Spirited children,
comfy old friends -
real conversations, where no-one pretends.

Freedom, to travel,
adequate wealth -
body in motion and excellent health.

Absence of chaos,
chakras aligned -
teachings, to nourish a curious mind.

Gossip averted,
prejudice free -
safe in the world being authentically me.

Kissable moments,
burning desires -
soul drenching music and crackling fires.

Dancing unbridled,
candles alight -
champagne and fairy lights twinkling at night.

Colours of autumn,
crunchable leaves -
springtime with blossoms, and beautiful trees.

Sunsets, and seashells,
feet in the sand -
sharing with someone; a hand in my hand.

Guidance from instinct,
aging, with grace -
laughter and memories etched on my face.

That's what I'm planning,
whatever life brings -
I feel more alive as I tick off these things.

The end

Thankyou

I'm deeply grateful you've come on this journey with me. Publishing a book of poetry has been a dream of mine since I was a child, so I'm excited it's become a reality. I hope to write many more, as I find myself constantly inspired by life with its surprising swirls and turns.

Thank you to all the people who have inspired me... the poets, philosophers, songwriters, musicians, and artists who have touched me with me their own work. I was delighted to see the works of Kahlil Gibran available in the public domain, which enabled me to use and give credit to his work in this book.

Thank you to all the friends in my life who have believed in my writing and in me (you know who you are). Thanks also to those who have followed me on social media and provided me with feedback that has given me the momentum to publish this book. I wouldn't have done this without you.

I would mean a lot to me if you could leave a book review on Amazon to let others know your thoughts about **The Lotus**. If you have a favourite poem or any resonate with you in particular, I'd love that feedback too. Thankyou.

Catherine Campbell

Printed in Great Britain
by Amazon

20618814R10068